LLYFRGELL CAERFYRDDIN
CARMARTHEN LIBRARY
Tynnwyd o'r stoc
Pris/Price
Withdrawn from stock

SCIENCE THROUGH THE SEASONS
SUMMER IN THE WOOD

SCIENCE THROUGH THE SEASONS

SUMMER IN THE WOOD

Janet Fitzgerald

Hamish Hamilton · London

Acknowledgement
I should like to express my gratitude to the schools, teachers and children with whom I have worked, and with whose help I have gained the experience and confidence needed to write this series. I am particularly indebted to those schools which allowed photographs to be taken as the children carried out their investigations. Thanks are also due to Chris Fairclough for some of the excellent photographs illustrating the texts. Finally, I am most grateful to my editors, Anna Sandeman and Sue Twiselton, for all their encouragement and professional advice.

Janet Fitzgerald

The author and publisher would also like to thank the following for permission to reproduce photographs: ARDEA pages 6 (both), 12, 14, 20 (bottom), 22; Bruce Coleman Limited pages 7 (all), 16, 23; NHPA cover (right), 8, 9, 13, 15, 18, 20 (top); OSF Picture Library pages 10; Tony Stone Worldwide page 24; Chris Fairclough cover (left) and pages 11, 17, 19, 21, 25.

First published in Great Britain 1987 by
Hamish Hamilton Children's Books
27 Wrights Lane, London W8 5TZ
Copyright © 1987 by Janet Fitzgerald
All rights reserved

British Library Cataloguing in Publication Data
Fitzgerald, Janet
Summer in the wood. – (Science through the seasons).
1. Summer – Juvenile literature
I. Title II. Series
574.5'43   QH81

ISBN 0–241–12094–2

Printed in Great Britain by
William Clowes Ltd, Beccles, Suffolk

Author's note

Books in this series are intended for use by young children actively engaged in exploring the environment in the company of a teacher or parent. Many lifelong interests are formed at this early age, and a caring attitude towards plants, animals and resources can be nurtured to become a mature concern for conservation in general.

The basis for all scientific investigation rests on the ability to observe closely and to ask questions. These books aim to increase a child's awareness so that he or she learns to make accurate observations. First-hand experience is encouraged and simple investigations of observations are suggested. The child will suggest many more! The aim is to give children a broad base of experience and 'memories' on which to build for the future.

Contents

Willowherb	6
Birds	8
Insects	10
Moss	12
Leaves	14
Caterpillars	16
Bees	18
Ants	20
Food	22
Walks	24
For teachers and parents	26
Extension activities	26
Index	29

It is Summer in the wood and willowherb grows tall.

What colour is willowherb?

Look at the shape of the flower.

Where are the flowers growing?

Look for three other flowers in the garden or school grounds.

Where did you find the flowers?

Draw a picture of them.

Why do flowers grow there?

It is Summer in the wood and the male cuckoo is calling.

Can you make the sound of a cuckoo calling?

The female cuckoo lays her eggs in a nest belonging to another bird.

This bird looks after the cuckoo chicks.

Stand outside and listen to the birds.

Can you make the sound of a bird calling?

This bird is seen in woods and gardens.

It has a gentle soft call.

It is Summer in the wood and insects are hatching.

Where will these insects live?

What do they like to eat?

These insects are sometimes eaten by other creatures.

Take a small container and look at the bark and leaves of a tree.

Can you see an insect?

Try to catch it.

Look closely at the insect in your container. How many legs has it got?

Does it have wings?

How does the insect move?

(Remember to put the insect back where it was found.
Then wash your hands.)

**It is Summer in the wood and
moss looks green on the tree stumps.**

Where does the moss like to grow?

Is they any moss near your house or school?

Where is your moss growing?

Collect a piece of moss from different places.

Draw the places where you found your moss. Look at the moss closely.

Is it all the same?

Look at the pictures. They are not the same.

How are they different?

It is Summer in the wood and leaves look shiny in the sunlight.

Look where the sunlight touches the leaves.

Are all the leaves turned towards the sun?

Draw the shape of a leaf.

Find six leaves with holes, torn edges, or marks.

Look carefully at the six leaves.

Look on top of each leaf and underneath it.

Draw the leaves, showing the holes and marks.

What could have caused these holes and marks?

It is Summer in the wood and caterpillars and insects are eating the leaves.

The caterpillars hatch when the sun is warm.

Where do the caterpillars hatch out?

Why is the wood a good place for caterpillars to live?

Collect two different caterpillars.

Also take some of the leaves they are eating.

Make the caterpillars a home you think they will like.

Watch them to see how they eat.

How do they move?

Are both caterpillars the same?

(Remember to put the caterpillars back where they were found. Then wash your hands.)

It is Summer in the wood and bees are working in the flowers.

Bees are very busy in Summer.

They visit flowers with bright colours.

What are the colours of the flower in this picture?

Look to see which flowers bees visit in the garden or school grounds.

Can you see what they are collecting?

They may be collecting pollen to take back to a hive.

What will the pollen be used for?

Be careful. Bees can sting!

It is Summer in the wood and wood ants are busy.

What shape is the wood ants' nest?

Where have the ants chosen to build their nest?

Don't go near wood ants as they can bite!

Find some garden ants. There may be black ants under stones.

Ask an adult to put some carefully into a clear container with a lid.

Look closely at the ants.

How many legs have they got?

How many parts has each ant's body got?

How do the ants move?

It is Summer in the wood and blue tits are collecting caterpillars.

The birds are feeding their young with caterpillars.

Where will the birds find the caterpillars?

Why is the wood a good place to look?

In the wood, all living things eat other living things.

Here are some creatures which live in the wood in Summer.

    ants   bees
    blue tits   ladybirds
    caterpillars greenfly
    voles

Can you find out what they eat and what eats them?

(Some of the answers are in this book.)

**It is Summer in the wood and
we can take walks, or eat a picnic.**

There are many things to see
and hear in a wood in Summer.

It is the time when all living
things are very busy.

When you go on a walk with your parents or your teacher, look and listen as you go.

Make a chart to show all the things you have seen.

Make another chart to show all the things you heard.

Did you notice any interesting smells?

For teachers and parents

We all recognise that children possess an insatiable curiosity about the rich environment and exciting experiences around them. For this reason they have a natural affinity for science and a basic inclination to explore and discover the world in which we live. We need to foster this sense of wonder by encouraging a scientific way of thinking in the early years. Children's own experience of the immediate environment will provide a natural starting point.

Through science children can evolve an active process of enquiry. This begins with observation (including sorting, comparing, ordering and measuring) and continues with asking questions, devising practical investigations, predicting outcomes, controlling variables, noting results, and perhaps modifying the original question in the light of discovery. The books in this series offer suggestions for engaging young children in this sort of active enquiry by relating seasonal change to familiar surroundings.

Extension activities

pp. 6–7
Find some willowherb and study it. Is the stem rough or smooth? Do the leaves have a smooth or jagged edge? Look out for the downy white willowherb seeds.

Try to discover which flowers grow in full sun, partial shade and deep shade. Is there a growth or colour pattern for each area? Compare different flowers of the same type, and with other types. Do they all have the same number of petals? Are the stalks the same? Do the stalks have thorns or prickles?

pp. 8–9
It is possible to distinguish different bird calls near the house or school. Doing this helps children develop their listening sense, which often remains underdeveloped. Children can also begin to sharpen their powers of observation by looking for specific characteristics of common garden birds, such as colour, shape and movement. Some birds stay in their own territorial areas, which may be observed in the garden or school grounds. Notes may be made of perching points, appearance times, flight patterns and feeding habits. Emphasise the importance of caring for birds and feeding them during the Winter months. No eggs must be disturbed and old nests must not be removed until late Autumn.

pp. 10–11
Distinguish between the shape, colour, size and habits of the insects you find. Encourage the children to notice the type of plant on which the insect is found. Is it eating the plant or just resting there? Do insects fly at all times of the day, in all kinds of weather? What creatures feed on insects? Are some insects useful?

pp. 12–13
If children look closely, they will notice that moss grows best in dark, damp conditions. Investigate what happens if moss is left in the sun or in a warm place, or if it is immersed in water. Close observation will help children to distinguish between algae, lichen, liverwort and moss. Find examples of these, and discover which conditions each needs for growth.

pp. 14–15
It is possible to identify those caterpillars and insects responsible for damage to plant stems and leaves. Find out if most damage occurs near the top, or bottom of a tree; on the outer, or inner leaves. Do some caterpillars and insects live on only one type of tree or bush? Is there a reason for this? Find out what happens to insects when trees and bushes lose their leaves.

pp. 16–17
Children are fascinated by caterpillars and nearly always want to collect them. This is a good time to stress the importance of conservation, and to ensure that after the children have watched and compared their caterpillars, they return the caterpillars to the wild to complete their life cycle. The importance of maintaining the correct balance of wild life can be emphasised.

Caterpillars vary so much in colour, size and shape that studying them is very rewarding. Look for a link between the colour of a caterpillar and the plant it is on. Look at the sucker pads on the underside of a caterpillar and watch how it uses them to help it move.

pp. 18–19
Observe the colour patterns of flowers which help to attract bees. Investigate the flower scents. Is there a relationship between colour and scent? Do flowers with strong scents attract most bees? Which colour/shape attracts most bees?

pp. 20–21
An ant house may be bought, made, or converted from a wormery, and for a short time ants may be kept here quite happily. Encourage children to watch ants' activities. Where do the ants go? Do they always follow the same routes? What do ants like to eat? Do ants respond to light or noise? Do ants like damp or dry conditions? Do ants care for each other? If one of your ants is a queen, it may be possible to keep the ants until after egg-laying, so allowing you to study their life cycle.

pp. 22–23
Much of the activity in a wood depends on the light and temperature these, and the food chains which have been established. Children who have been observing and caring for living things will soon become interested in the whole pattern of life in a wood. This is the time to introduce them to the idea of interdependence in nature. Taking one tree as an example, encourage them to work out what the tree needs in order to survive, and which animals and plants need the tree in order to live.

pp. 24–25
Using the environment as a resource is often a good way of integrating different areas of learning. Communicating what is observed through language or writing is one way of recording the experience. Recording by means of measurement, charts or artwork is another possibility. Sharing an experience with others can sharpen observation and lead to questions. These may be followed up with further investigations.

INDEX

ants   20, 21, 23

bark   11
bees   18, 23
birds   8, 9, 22
blue tits   22, 23

caterpillars   16, 17, 22, 23
chicks   8
colours   18
cuckoo   8

eggs   8

feedings   22
flowers   6, 7, 18, 19

greenfly   23

insects   10, 11, 16

ladybirds   23
leaves   11, 14, 15, 16, 17

moss   12, 13

nests   8, 20

shapes   7, 14
sun   14, 16
sunlight   14

trees   11
tree stumps   12

voles   23

walks   24, 25
willowherb   6, 7
wood ants   20

۲